SISI AND THE GIRL FROM TOWN

poems by

Jessica Jewell

Finishing Line Press
Georgetown, Kentucky

SISI AND THE GIRL FROM TOWN

Copyright © 2019 by Jessica Jewell
ISBN 978-1-63534-995-5 First Edition
All rights reserved under International and Pan-American Copyright Conventions. No part of this book may be reproduced in any manner whatsoever without written permission from the publisher, except in the case of brief quotations embodied in critical articles and reviews.

ACKNOWLEDGMENTS

American Poetry Journal: "Sisi on the Banks of the Würmsee"
A Narrow Fellow: "End of Blackberry Season"
Anemone Sidecare: "The Ancient City's Sunflower Farmer"
Cider Press Review: "How the Balaton Wine Survived"
Tahoma Literary Review: "Summer at the Horgoš Border Crossing"
The Adirondack Review: "By Looking, I Take it In"

Publisher: Leah Maines
Editor: Christen Kincaid
Cover Art and Design: Sebastian Giraldo Gabiria
Author Photo: Györgyi Mihályi-Jewell

Printed in the USA on acid-free paper.
Order online: www.finishinglinepress.com
also available on amazon.com

Author inquiries and mail orders:
Finishing Line Press
P. O. Box 1626
Georgetown, Kentucky 40324
U. S. A.

Table of Contents

The Balaton Wine Survived 1

Sisi on the Banks of the Würmsee 2

The End of Blackberry Season 33

Tracks 4

Death of the Robber King 5

Sisi and the Marriage of Convenience 6

High Culture 7

The Fog and Leaf Fire 8

The Ancient City's Sunflower Farmer 9

Sisi in her Youth 10

Sisi and the Gift 11

Sisi Sets the Fire 12

Summer at the Horgoš Border Crossing 13

By Looking I Take It In 14

The Ages 15

They Murdered Our Queen 16

Elisabeth Amalie Eugenie von Wittelsbach (Sisi), Empress consort of Austria, Apostolic Queen consort of Hungary, Queen consort of Bohemia and Croatia, was born on December 24, 1837 in the Kingdom of Bavaria. She was assassinated on September 10, 1898 while on holiday in Switzerland.

...*The natural destiny of a Queen is to give an heir to the throne. If the Queen is so fortunate as to provide the State with a Crown-Prince this should be the end of her ambition – she should by no means meddle with the government of an Empire, the care of which is not a task for women... If the Queen bears no sons, she is merely a foreigner in the State, and a very dangerous foreigner, too.*

—from a pamphlet given to Queen Elisabeth from her mother-in-law, Princess Sophie of Bavaria

THE BALATON WINE SURVIVED

Most of the soil takes in the seeds
and what are left darken
into the volcanic loam. One sunbeam
each for the sprouts. The wind empties
out of the lake and climbs the sharp
hillsides. At the top, the church bell
announces Sunday lunch. Startled,
Ágnes Varga drops the bowl of peas.
Something you might call happiness
is happening now. A century ago
every vine from here to Szekszárd
was nibbled away by the phylloxera bugs.
This was before the Queen was murdered.
Before the bombings left wide gapes
in the monastic cellars and most of the village
men were sent to the front. Before
widows and mothers who mourned them
had nothing left to nourish but a grape.

SISI ON THE BANK OF WÜRMSEE

I buoy into the water one skin
lighter than the blue color of night.
A yellow bird sleeps on the edge
of driftwood. Under the moon
it takes the shape of a closed lily.
The wind and the sound of it
passes the bald cherry trees.
Joyful and young, I recall the smell
of the zither strings and its wood
on my father's fingers. His hair
was full of the sun's orange feathers.

Before the night they found Ludwig
floating dead, elbows lodged deep
into the shore mud, my father was more
or less a happy man, the type to believe
in happiness. Had happiness worked,
or love, I would still be here, my first
home, floating on its surface like ribbon.

END OF BLACKBERRY SEASON
Nógrád

This morning the rooster's lungs strain
a cockled melody as if late summer
sets on his vocal chords. In the fields,
the fattened blackberry buds bow to the grass,
and the honeybees nearly stand on their heads
suckling the pink nectar wingside. Inside
everyone is sleeping, as are the farm workers
and the mare who needs tending in the barn.

The village dogs that spent the night
moon-howling rest now in thin alleys
of dawn, though the intercity train
briefly disturbs their dreams of running.

A Tin Heron nests on the gunpowder ruins

above the cellars someone carved into the hills,
half a century ago
to protect the wine from the bombs.

TRACKS

The train steams north toward Donovaly and the pine-
jeweled slopes of the Veľká Fatr. Black forest stalks
form a latched awning over the tracks. Blackened
wheat lie in piles under broken-limb transformers,
pout in the sleeping farmland that even the Black
Grouse, Bean Goose and Gadwalls have forgotten.

I wonder whose fire belongs to the smoke crowning
the village proper. The endless Carpathian snow pillows
the pine trees in Kassa's unswept courtyards.
The steam rises, but is caught by cones, falls back

to the dead nettles. The snow banks are breathing, see?

We buy a highway ticket and a Coke from Slovnaft station.
Snow on the tracks. The sound of rumbling steel
echoes a gentle tenor for miles. Through mountains

and fog that hangs as rough as homemade curtains,
a sunray—light through the needled and bent conifers.

And you, dog, crossing there on the rusted bridge, leave
your paw-tracks for the children to follow in the morning
like tiny Sherlocks. Leave the world its clues to follow
you, like you follow the lung-bark call of some master.

DEATH OF THE ROBBER KING

> *The Hungarian papers announced the death, in the prison of Szamos-Újvár, of the celebrated bandit Sándor Rózsa, known in Hungary as the "robber-King." His generosity toward the poor, and his gallantry toward women made him a sort of national hero.*
> —New York Times, December 15, 1878

Her favorite place to hide was Ludas lake.
Summer-loved, once, she hid from him
among the wide-mouthed inlet beds formed
a million years ago by wind running its chops
over the plains. She hid but it's a game she played.
He was known around town for mischief,
for being a lurch. He was known as a father
and once for gallantry and once for stealing silver
and stealing horses and stealing kisses
and summers. She hid there, among the summer
reeds. Charted stars. Charted months by blooming
lax-flowered orchids in the lowlands, periwinkle
nibbled down by duck and otter. After his arrest,
someone cut the tail off her calf. She mourned
the motherless but not the milk. Summer-loved,
once, but not after, when love was a quantity
of waiting. The reeds, bars. The wind, webs.
The snapped duck and all that winter down.

SISI AND A MARRIAGE OF CONVENIENCE

You did it as a means
to an end and then it ended
and you spent all your nights
and a few dawns too
fishing your voice for chords.
So many people loved you
died and it wasn't even
a time of uprisings.
All you could think about
were trains and riverbeds
and exercise regimes
and a wolf at your gate
and father who adored you
more than your sister
and let you ride gypsy
and taught you to lie.
Someone named a castle
after you, and a cake,
and a thousand and more
daughters. But had they
known what you saw
when you looked in the
glass they would have
covered every mirror
in their city apartments
and thrashed at a century
of nights to forget you, you
knew the sound of assassin,
you couldn't warn them, you
took the knife to save them too.

HIGH CULTURE

In the lower worlds, where all things are slowed but not gone, they take the old diseases and give them new names. Suffering is a human cholera. It takes the nape of a child. Turns the skin in on itself. It is known as the Skeleton Age. In the Age of Drought, who are you to question water's holiness? Dip two fingers in. Take it to the forehead, chest, shoulder to shoulder. Take a rapid by the mouth and see if it is a blessing then. On the Great Plain, half the Steppe cattle died this winter. Herds once in the millions that survived since prehistory on the grasses wasted down to their hooves. This was known as The Hunger. Or, animals of instinct, they simply left us. The Steam Age and Vanishing and Burial rising over their hides like claws.

THE FOG AND THE LEAF FIRE

The afternoon we drive toward Sisi's country
home to buy the new car, the sky abandons clouds
all around us. No rain falls, fog has limped in layers
for days. Strange for November & the Carpathian shell.

Pensioner widowers holed-up in weekend homes
for winter burn leaf piles on the side of the road.

The smell of the burning—carbon, humic, metals
linger on my tonsils. All that night I toss thinking
about Hungary's favorite Queen, her sadness,
how nothing cures a bad taste once its inside you.

Years ago, in the Rust Belt, the neighbor man raked
the brittle copper and xanthous dead into piles,
and always the sound: gash of metal against grass.

I watched him autumn weekends from the rock stairs
where my babysitter's brother split his head open
in a bicycle accident one summer. He was ten
years old and on his way to the Dairy Queen.

For days I tried to spit out the taste of the burning.
I remember spitting. And I never thought about
it until the afternoon on the way to Gödöllő. The fog.
Blood-stained rock. That man raking the ground bald.

THE ANCIENT CITY'S SUNFLOWER FARMER

> *As the ancients of the city pass away, who will keep the testimony burning...?*
> —Shaker Elderess Anna White

My shadow climbs out of the river
onto the path of the dam. A farmer
in his morning industry gazes
at the waking sunflower fields.
His water pup pants next to him,
has been swimming too, all dawn
long, and the evening before chasing
every horned stag and hornless fawn.

He shifts his glance to the glass eye
of the river, where I have curled
in from, but ignores me and every
other sound. The coterie of teenage
revelers lurching out from the cafe
at the bridge. Slovakian boys
pronouncing last chance invitations
in unverbed, untensed English
to the Hungarian girls already on
their way, already back in their father's
homes. Mist circles the sunflowers
like a necklace of clouded crystals.

My shadow falls out of the river
and onto the path of the dam. I run toward
this priest of pastures, but he does
not look at me, nor does he acknowledge
the drag of the Olympic boat crews
on the muddied Tisza, the clop and breath
of morning riders, the creak of bicycles
carrying outland villagers to market.

He is nearly a century old. Knows
invasions. And I am as early as a flood.

SISI IN HER YOUTH

Spent summers peering over edges.
The stone bridge deep in the marsh
and the creek beds glazed with chestnuts
and summer vines. On the hill above the bridge,
a runoff hungered down the mud slope looking
for a place to pool. She called it a waterfall.
Some summers there was little more
than a plane of water, soft as a nibble
on the leaves. Some years the creek
was deep enough to stretch and swim.

Sisi and the girl from town, the one
her mother warned her about, dropped
from the vines and into the water
until their happiness was evening's architect
and the whole kingdom, a single heartbeat.

Some years later, when asked about love,
the Queen looked back—over the lip
of the bridge where she saw the whole forest
trembling—the breast and the vine. The collarbone
and lobe and gully. The rosy tongue
of that forgotten edge, rolling her name.

SISI AND THE GIFT

A lynx took the lamb
at night, though no one heard the wail.

By morning, the blood had pooled,
half-body, speckled by teeth,
abandoned in a red ribbon,
meat spilling from bone.

You see it heaped there, the lamb
spoiling in the sun, her curls
of white and gray hair caught
in the up-drift wind. Far from here,

in the cities, all the thinking
is about domestication. To breed away
the primitive, evolve beyond the cave.

As if satisfaction can be trained.

SISI SETS THE FIRE

> *Ein Unergründlich tiefer See*
> *Ist meine Seele,*
> *Den ich oft selber nicht versteh*
>
> *The endless lake*
> *Is my soul:*
> *I see no sense in it.*
>
> —Elisabeth of Bavaria, Empress of Austria,
> Queen of Hungary, Croatia, and Bohemia

I set fire to the lake. I burn
the oars of the gunboat.
I singe my fingers—the tips
like blackened charcoaled cotton bolls.
I take my soul as the immeasurable.
The lake is gone. The fire is gone.
The me and the once I was happy here.
The flame is the red pool forming
from the gum of each extraction.
Mouthless woman. Voiceless one.

SUMMER AT THE HORGOŠ BORDER CROSSING

I missed her body, and I cried about her body
and I found myself on the carpet knocking
my fists around. I missed her lips, and I cried
about her lips, and I found myself at the mirror
plotting out ways of breaking the law. I missed
her hair, and I cried about the smell of soap
that I could not replicate on my own,
or the sheets or the pillow or the dog. I missed her
eyes, and I cried about her eyes. I missed her plots,
and I found myself acting them out. I discovered
in myself the old key the old radical the old coffee
drinker hollering death threats to the empire
and allies and the Bolsheviks too. I found in myself
the old country and the map she drew for me.
I dreamt only of ghosts and bandits and the Carpathian
plains flooding toward her on wind and wings.

BY LOOKING I TAKE IT IN

Halfway to Szeged from Budapest
I see the mare in the wheat field.
Mustang blood, oxide brown, pom.
I wish her to be napping in that daisy
pasture, dreaming of her first master
or of Sisi in her youth, or the last
bucket of carrots flavored with rain.
Death is hard to imagine here, when water
is on its way, when there hasn't been
a barn fire in years, when the vet
is just up the road. Behind the cellars,
roosters are leaving tracks. Two Polski
Fiats erode on cinderblocks. There's a boy
in the yard. He has a jar of ticks he tore off
the dogs, blood or dirt rust his cheeks.
Bed sheets, linens, jerk the line. Smoke
rises like an up-drift inking of the heavens.

These are not the days of famine, but here,
in this Carpathian field, a dead horse.

And in the horse the whole of the Carpathians—

its basin and its lowlands and loam, and the brows
of its conquerors, riding home. And the kings
and women who bedded them. In this field
and its unsettled grains, the late rain and thirst.

THE AGES

They called the last one the Age of Missing. *I miss you,* they heard themselves saying, though it was a kind of lie, or worse, relief, like the abandoned shoes at the bottom of the Danube, or that gift the river made depositing them on the banks of the city islands, decades after the armies invaded and the children lost them and the whole district was sent to the camps. In the Age of Empty Rooms, a woman heard those ghosts screaming for her, thought it was the sound of spiders weaving their silks in the unopened doorways of the city flat, bare of her stolen tapestries and family. In the old countries they know that vanishing is not the beginning or end of ages. Invaders comes through the plains and farms and villages, leave their poisons, take the women, kill the horses and dogs, leave the resistors snout-first in the first spring fields for a slow lunch of stripped poppies. Some call that the Age of Beginnings or the Age of the Christian Kings. The rest know the truth—one age begets the next and always ends in the place they are always trying to escape, this, the Age of Outlands.

THEY MURDERED OUR QUEEN

—Hungarian newspaper "Magyar Hírlap" on September 10, 1898

Poor Countess Sztáray, clumsy with ties

of a bloody corset. Clumsy boatmen
who carried me through the quay
in the ship's sail to my death bed
in the Hôtel Beau-Rivage.

On the dock, three women stuff their faces
with French creams.

In the water, a dead swan.
Feathers shucked off by lightning.

You could say I was sensitive to animals
since an early age riding gypsy
bareback on my mares. Sensitive
to the telegraph's unoiled metal
arms, ricketing unwanted news.

Father's in Egypt again.
Mother's made other arrangements for my love.
Body of the boat deck, squealing back to shore.
Body of the newsboy starving for stares.

Body tedium, daffy and aching
jaw of an Italian woman, not even mine,
too young for courtesy, mispronouncing my name.

Jessica Jewell is the author of three collections of poetry including *Slap Leather* (dancing girl press) and *Dust Runner* (forthcoming from Finishing Line Press). She is currently the senior academic program director for the Wick Poetry Center at Kent State University, where she also earned her PhD in higher education administration and MFA in poetry. Her academic writing has been published most recently in the *Journal of Comparative and International Higher Education* and *Inside Higher Education*. Her poetry has appeared in *Cider Press Review*, *American Poetry Journal*, and *Nimrod* among others. Jewell lives in northeast Ohio with her wife and two gorgeous dogs.

www.ingramcontent.com/pod-product-compliance
Lightning Source LLC
LaVergne TN
LVHW041526070426
835507LV00013B/1847